FUELING THE FUTURE

Wind Energy

Elizabeth Raum

Heinemann Library
Chicago, Illinois

Photo research by Rebecca Sodergren and Hannah Taylor
Illustrations by Jeff Edwards
Designed by Richard Parker and Q2A Solutions
Originated by Chroma Graphics (Overseas) Pte Ltd
Printed and bound in China by Leo Paper Group

12 11 10 09 08
10 9 8 7 6 5 4 3 2 1

Library of Congress Cataloging-in-Publication Data
Raum, Elizabeth.
  Wind energy / Elizabeth Raum.
    p. cm. -- (Fueling the future)
  Includes bibliographical references and index.
  ISBN 978-1-4329-1566-7 (hc) -- ISBN 978-1-4329-1572-8 (pb) 1. Wind power--Juvenile literature. I. Title.
  TJ820.R38 2008
  333.9'2--dc22
                        2007050865

Acknowledgments
The author and publisher are grateful to the following for permission to reproduce
copyright material: ©Alamy pp. **4** (John Martin), **8** (Robert Harding Picture Library Ltd); ©Atkins Bahrain
p. **14**; ©Camera Press London p. **16** (Gamma, Raphael Gaillarde); ©Corbis pp. **5** (Ludovic Maisant), **15**
(Paul A. Souders), **25** (Brooks Kraft); ©Eyevine p. **26** (Redux/Mark Leong); ©Getty Images pp. **12** (Justin
Sullivan), **20** (AFP/Jim Russi); ©Greenpeace p. **21**; ©Hydro Tasmania p. **18**; ©PA Photos p. **6** (AP); ©Pela-
mis Wave Power p. **23**; ©SkySails p. **17**; ©Still Pictures pp. **10**, **13** (Paul Glendell), **19** (M. Henning); ©Wind
Power Co Ltd p. **27**.

Cover photograph of a wind turbine reproduced with permission of ©Photolibrary.com/Stockbyte. Cover
background image of blue virtual whirl reproduced with permission of ©istockphoto.com/Andreas
Guskos.

The publishers would like to thank David Hood of the Centre for Alternative Technology for his assistance
in the preparation of this book.

Contents

Some words are shown in bold, **like this**. You can find out what they mean by looking in the glossary.

Energy is the ability to do work. Energy is what makes things move or change. Sailboats move across the water because they use the wind's energy. River rafts float down the river because they use the energy of moving water. Anything in motion has a form of energy called **kinetic energy**.

Energy cannot be destroyed, but it can be changed from one form to another. Most of the Earth's energy comes from the sun. This energy is called **solar energy**. We use solar energy every day. The sun warms the Earth and gives us light. But the sun's energy also takes other forms. For example, a tree **absorbs** (takes in) solar energy. It uses some of the solar energy to grow and stores the rest in its wood. If the tree is later used for firewood, the stored energy from the sun produces heat when the wood is burned.

This ship depends on wind to move it across the ocean.

This ocean liner, one of the world's largest, gets its energy from fossil fuels.

Why do we need energy?

Humans depend on energy. Energy makes the wind blow and rain fall from the sky. Energy makes plants grow. Plants provide food for animals and people. The food gives us the energy we need to live.

But we also use energy in more complicated ways. We use energy to heat and light our houses. We use energy to run factories and to run cars, trains, and airplanes. We usually call this energy **fuel** or power.

Wanting more and more energy

Worldwide the need for energy keeps growing. Scientists expect the world's energy use to double every 35 years. This means that 35 years from today, the world will be using twice as much energy as we are using today. Where will we get energy in the future?

Fossil fuels

Today, most of the world's energy comes from **fossil fuels** called coal, oil, and **natural gas**. These fuels formed millions of years ago from the remains of plants and animals. Most fossil fuels are found underground or underwater.

Burning coal for energy sends pollution into the air.

Problems with fossil fuels

Fossil fuels **pollute** (dirty) the Earth, the oceans, and the air. Burning fossil fuels sends dangerous chemicals into the air. Fossil fuels are not **renewable**. They will not replace themselves over time. Some scientists believe that if people continue to use oil at today's rates, we will use up the world's oil supply in 40 to 60 years.

What is global warming?

The **greenhouse effect** is the rise in the Earth's temperature caused when certain gases, called **greenhouse gases**, trap energy from the sun. These gases (water vapor, **carbon dioxide**, **methane**, and others) let the sun's rays in, but prevent warm air from escaping into the **atmosphere**. The greenhouse effect keeps the Earth warm enough to support life.

However, in the last 100 years the Earth's average temperature has increased by about 1 °F (0.6 °C.) It may increase even faster during the next 100 years. Scientists call this temperature rise "global warming." They say that our use of fossil fuels is to blame. Burning fossil fuels increases the amount of greenhouse gases in the air. If the Earth's temperature continues to increase, the Earth's **climate** may change in disastrous ways. For example, higher temperatures may cause the polar icecaps to melt, flooding land along the coasts.

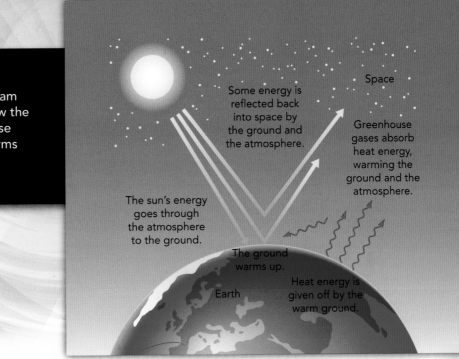

This diagram shows how the greenhouse effect warms the Earth.

Some energy is reflected back into space by the ground and the atmosphere.

Space

Greenhouse gases absorb heat energy, warming the ground and the atmosphere.

The sun's energy goes through the atmosphere to the ground.

The ground warms up.

Earth

Heat energy is given off by the warm ground.

Looking for alternative fuels

To meet the world's energy needs, we must find **alternative** fuels. They must be renewable fuels that replace themselves over time. We will need fuels that do not pollute the Earth or cause **global warming**.

What Is Wind Energy?

People have used wind **energy** for thousands of years. In ancient Egypt, people used wind energy to sail boats on the Nile River. Ancient people in Asia invented windmills and used them to pump water and grind grain. By the 1100s, people in Europe were using windmills, too. Over the years, windmills changed. People invented different kinds of blades to provide greater power.

People began using wind to **generate** (make) electricity in the late 1800s. By 1889 there were 77 windmill companies in the United States. Windmills were used on the Great Plains of the United States to supply electricity until the late 1920s, when electric power lines reached the area.

Windmills like this one were used throughout Europe to pump water and to grind grain into flour.

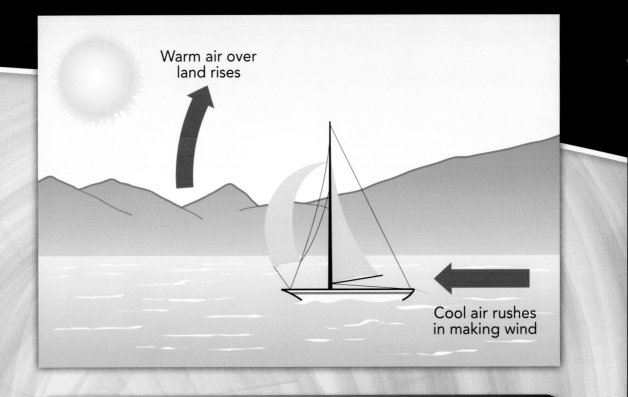

Warm air over land rises

Cool air rushes in making wind

What causes wind?

Wind is moving air. The sun heats the Earth unevenly, and this causes winds. Different types of land and water **absorb** the sun's heat differently. For example, land heats up more quickly than water, so the warm air over land rises. Cooler air over the water rushes in to take its place (see diagram). Water takes longer to warm up, but it stays warm longer. So at night, the warm air over the water rises, and the cooler air over the land rushes in to take its place.

Why choose wind today?

Wind energy is the fastest-growing source of **renewable** energy in the world. Unlike **fossil fuels**, we will not run out of wind. Wind does not **pollute**. It does not give off **greenhouse gases** that cause **global warming**. Wind is free and it is available all over the world. In many ways, wind is an ideal energy source for the future.

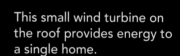

This small wind turbine on the roof provides energy to a single home.

How do we capture the wind?

To use wind energy, we need **turbines**. Most modern wind turbines have blades similar to those of old-fashioned windmills. Wind turns the blades around a **rotor**. The rotor connects to a main shaft that spins a **generator** to make electricity. To capture the wind, wind turbines are usually at least 100 feet (30 meters) above the ground. If a turbine is too low to the ground, trees and buildings may slow the winds down so that they cannot produce enough energy to run the generator.

Some homeowners put turbines on their roofs or in their yards to provide electricity for their own house. These turbines may provide enough electricity to run the refrigerator and small appliances. However, they may not be powerful enough to meet all the family's energy needs.

Who's using wind energy?

Germany, Denmark, and Spain lead the world in using wind energy. In Germany, more than 4 percent of the country's electricity comes from wind power. More than 6 percent of Spain's energy needs come from wind energy. Denmark gets around 20 percent of its electric power from wind. These countries hope to increase their use of wind energy.

Use of wind energy is growing worldwide. About 1.5 million homes are added each year to the number of homes using wind energy. In the United States, less than 1 percent of electric power comes from wind. But the number is increasing. Soon the United States will have over three million homes running on wind energy. The United Kingdom is planning several major **wind farms** that will provide energy to homes along the coastline.

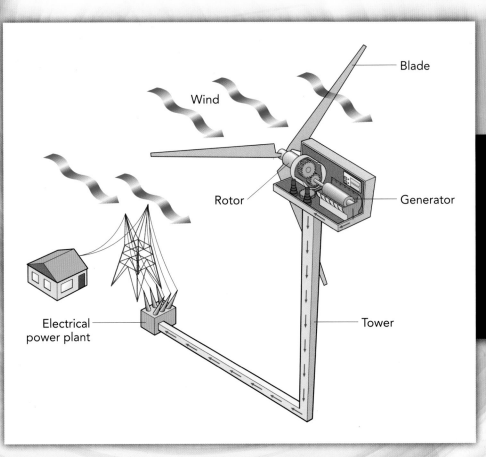

Blade

Wind

Rotor

Generator

Electrical power plant

Tower

This model shows the parts of a wind turbine. The wind (arrows) turns the giant blades that turn the generator, which makes electricity.

What Is a Wind Farm?

It takes many large **turbines** to provide enough electricity to meet the needs of an entire community or region. Many large turbines linked together form a **wind farm**. Almost all of the wind **energy** used in Europe and North America comes from large wind farms.

The turbines used on wind farms are called **utility-scale turbines**. Some are over 40 stories tall. Their propeller-like blades are as long as two jumbo jets. Wind farms require a lot of space.

Wind farms can be located on land or in the ocean off the coast. Offshore wind farms **generate** up to 50 percent more energy than wind farms on land, but they are more costly to build.

The amount of energy a wind turbine captures depends on the size of the blades and the strength of the wind.

The first offshore wind farm was built in 1991 in Denmark. Offshore wind farms, like this one in Wales, generate more energy than those on land.

Offshore wind farms

To build an offshore wind farm, workers drive piles, heavy beams that support the tower, deep into the seabed. They place a foundation on top of the piles and build the turbine tower on top of the foundation. The foundation is painted a bright color so that ships will see it. Long cables beneath the sea take electric power to the shore where it is connected to the electricity supply for the country.

World's biggest wind farms

The Horse Hollow Wind Energy Center in Texas operates 421 wind turbines on 47,000 acres of land. It can power 230,000 homes.

New buildings

Some **engineers** are using wind energy in the design of new buildings. When the island country of Bahrain, located in the Middle East, decided to build a new World Trade Center, engineers considered including **renewable** energy. The building has two sail-shaped towers with three wind turbines balanced between them. The turbines are specially designed to increase the wind speed and generate enough wind energy to supply power to the building. There are proposals for similar buildings in other cities. Tall buildings in windy cities may be able to use wind energy for day-to-day power needs.

This new building in Bahrain has wind turbines built between its towers.

What's Good About Wind Energy?

Wind **energy** is renewable. Wind speeds may vary from day to day, but there will always be wind. Wind blows almost everywhere on the Earth. Wind itself costs nothing, although the machines to turn it into usable energy can be expensive. Experts say that the cost is always highest when scientists and engineers are developing new programs. Over time, the costs come down. Eighty percent of the cost of a **wind farm** is in the machinery. Once the wind **turbines** are up and running, costs will be very low.

This wind farm uses Darrieus turbines to capture wind energy from all directions.

Darrieus turbine

The Darrieus turbine, which looks like a giant eggbeater, has four curved blades that turn around an upright tube. It works well no matter what direction the wind blows. **Vertical axis wind turbines**, like the Darrieus, come in various shapes and sizes. Today vertical wind turbines can be used on the tops of buildings and houses.

No pollution

Wind energy does not **pollute** or add **greenhouse gases** to the **atmosphere**. Wind turbines are able to capture between 20 percent and 40 percent of the energy in the wind and convert it to electricity or other uses. They do this without the risk of changing the **climate** or damaging our health.

Many experts believe that wind farms use the Earth wisely. Wind farms can be built on land that is currently not in use. Mountaintops or land too rough for farming can be used to produce wind energy. Offshore wind farms located far out to sea do not block the view, nor do they harm sea life. These wind farms are identified on shipping maps and are brightly colored, so they do not pose a danger to ships.

Wind farms can be built on land that is not useful for farming.

When ships use sails like these, they need less fossil fuel.

Wind saves fuel

New systems being developed by companies in Germany and Denmark may reduce the **fossil fuel** that large ships use by half. The new system uses giant sails to help pull heavy ships through the water. When the wind is blowing, the ships speed along without fossil fuel. They can use the sails alone or in combination with their engines. Either way saves energy. When the wind dies down, they rely on fossil fuel.

Does wind energy change our climate?

The word "climate" refers to weather observed over a long period of time in a particular place or region. Wind energy does not cause **global warming** or change the Earth's climate. However, the wind itself is part of our day-to-day weather. Without wind, the weather would not change much from day to day.

The biggest problem with wind **energy** is that the wind does not always blow. When there is no wind or the wind speed is low, wind **turbines** cannot **generate** energy. We need energy all the time. So if the wind is not blowing, we must find other energy sources. Until recently there was no way to store wind energy.

Now scientists in Australia have developed a new kind of battery that can store wind energy. On days when the wind is strong, the battery stores energy for use on days when there is not much wind.

Too much wind also poses a danger to wind turbines. Turbines must be built well to survive hurricanes, tornadoes, and other major storms.

Scientists at this wind farm in Australia are working to design a way to store wind energy.

Wind energy won't work everywhere

Some areas simply aren't suited to wind energy. People living in low wind areas will have to find other types of **alternative** energy to meet their needs. Scientists now believe that the best locations for **wind farms** are over the ocean, along coastal areas, and on high ridges.

Danger to birds?

About 40,000 birds are killed each year by wind turbines. **Engineers** are designing new, slower-moving turbines to help solve the problem. However, wind energy experts point out that birds face far greater dangers. For example, every year about 60 to 80 million birds are killed when they fly into cars.

Wind turbines pose a danger to birds.

What about the view?

Some people feel that wind turbines are ugly. They don't want to look at turbines or live near them. This is why some countries are putting wind turbines far offshore where they cannot be seen. Often land turbines are put up in areas far from towns and cities.

What Is Wave Energy?

When the wind blows over the ocean, it causes powerful waves. **Wave energy**, like all **energy**, begins with the sun. The uneven heating of the Earth produces wind, and that wind produces waves. Like wind, waves are a **renewable** energy source. Oceans cover almost three-quarters of the Earth's surface, and all oceans have waves. Learning how to use the waves to make energy is an important step in finding renewable **fuels** for the future. Several countries are working on ways to use the energy created by ocean waves.

Powerful waves carry surfers in to shore. Waves contain kinetic energy.

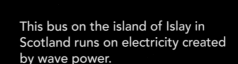

This bus on the island of Islay in Scotland runs on electricity created by wave power.

Wave energy is renewable energy. There is an endless supply of waves. Unlike wind energy, waves change very slowly. Waves are much more steady and predictable than winds. Wave energy, like wind energy, does not **pollute** the air. It does not cause **greenhouse gases**. Waves are free, so wave energy is less expensive than **fossil fuels**. However, **engineers** are still developing new tools, or **technologies**, to capture wave energy. It may be expensive to develop the technology for wave energy stations and to set them up, but once they are up and running, wave energy will be an inexpensive source of electricity.

The world's first wave energy station

The world's first wave energy station opened in 2000 on Islay Island off the coast of Scotland. The station is known as Limpet 500. It provides electricity to 400 homes. However, like wind farms, it has faced complaints about noise and how the station spoils the view.

How is wave energy captured?

Like wind energy, wave energy requires a **turbine**. Some turbines are deep underwater, while others ride on the waves. The turbine is connected to a **generator** that produces electricity. Wave energy can provide heat and light to houses, run small machines, and even power electric vehicles.

Wave energy will be most useful near the coasts. The United Kingdom and Portugal are in the process of building wave energy farms. In the United States, coastal cities are considering wave energy. Wave energy is so new that the systems are still being developed.

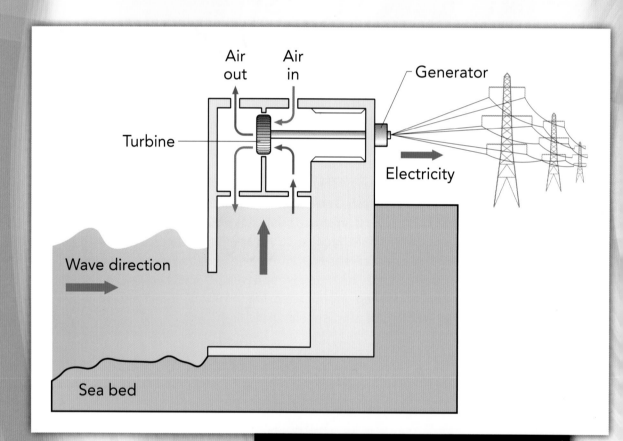

This diagram shows how one kind of wave turbine, the Limpet 500, works.

What would a wave farm look like?

Wave farms, like wind farms, would use hundreds of wave turbines to provide electricity to an entire city or region. Waves lose their power as they crash into the coast, so putting the wave farms 3 to 6 miles (5 to 10 kilometers) offshore would provide greater wave energy. Wave farms would be clearly marked on shipping maps so that boats would not hit the turbines. Scientists do not think the wave farms will cause problems for sea creatures.

These long snakelike machines will soon be used to provide wave energy in Portugal. Each one is about four train cars in length.

Wave energy in Portugal

Portugal is building the world's first wave farm. It will provide electricity for about 1,500 homes. Portugal hopes to increase the project to serve 15,000 homes in the future. The project uses the turbines pictured above. Waves enter the chamber and turn the **rotor**, which sends energy to a generator. These turbines are built to survive storms and to provide a steady flow of energy to the **electric grid**.

Wind **energy** and **wave energy** are promising sources of energy for the future. Scientists and **engineers** are working to make better wind **turbines** that spin at a slower speed while producing even more energy. In the future, wind turbines may look even stranger than the Darrieus turbine (see page 15), but they will do a better job of capturing wind energy.

In the future, people on cruise ships may notice many large **wind farms** far out at sea. They may have to look through the large sails on their ship to see the wind farms, but these sails will reduce the use of **fossil fuels** on the ship.

Countries such as India and China will greatly increase their use of wind energy in the future. These countries are eager to find energy that does not **pollute** the air. The United States and the United Kingdom also have wind energy projects underway.

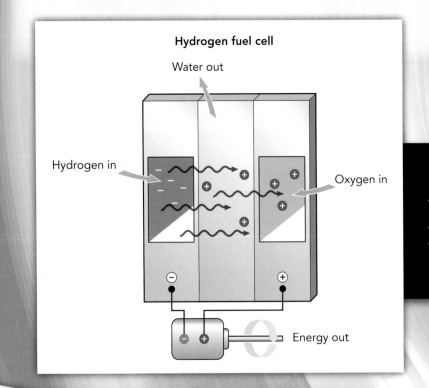

Hydrogen fuel cell

Water out

Hydrogen in

Oxygen in

Energy out

A hydrogen fuel cell is a kind of battery that uses hydrogen to provide energy.

This experimental car runs on hydrogen fuel cells instead of gasoline.

Wind-powered cars?

So far, most wind energy is used to produce electricity. But scientists believe that wind can also make **hydrogen**, a gas that can be used to store and transport energy. Scientists are developing batteries called **hydrogen fuel cells** that run on hydrogen **fuel**. In the future, hydrogen fuel cells could replace gasoline as a fuel for cars and buses. It is possible that wind energy will be used to make the fuel cells.

Hydrogen postal van

In 2004, the United States Postal Service (USPS) began using a hydrogen-powered van to deliver the mail in Washington, D.C. It was part of an experiment to test how well hydrogen-powered cars would work. The USPS was so pleased that it has extended the experiment to Irvine, California. The USPS, which drives 1.2 billion miles (1.9 billion kilometers) a year, is eager to find an **alternative** to expensive fossil fuels.

Searching for answers

People all over the world are searching for ways to replace fossil fuels. Wind energy and wave energy may be answers. Some experts believe that by the year 2050, one-third of the world's energy will be supplied by wind. Wind energy is **renewable**, inexpensive, and available in most places. Wind energy does not pollute. It does not give off **greenhouse gases**.

Inventors are finding new ways to use wind and waves every day. Some students in India found a way to use wind energy to power a cell phone. Another inventor designed a tiny wind turbine that can be put on the handlebar of a bicycle. As it turns, it provides enough energy to run a bicycle light. A student in Australia put sails on his skateboard. He crossed Australia using the sails.

China plans to produce 10 percent of its energy from renewable sources, such as wind, by 2020.

These tiny wind turbines provide enough energy to keep a bicycle light burning brightly.

A growing energy source

Wind energy is the fastest-growing energy source in the world. In 2006, the United States, Germany, India, Spain, and China nearly doubled their use of wind energy. Brazil had the biggest increase: it used seven times more wind energy in 2006 than it did in 2005. France, Canada, Portugal, and the United Kingdom also expanded their use of wind energy.

Even people without wind turbines use wind energy every day to sail boats, fly kites, and dry clothes. The wind dries the grass after a rainy day so we can play outside. The wind cools us in summer and brings fresh clean air into our homes all year long. Perhaps someday soon the wind will provide the energy to run our refrigerators, to light our homes, and to provide heat in the winter.

Wind Speed Map

This map shows wind speeds throughout the world. Notice that the strongest winds are located over the oceans. Where are the lowest wind speeds? Find your region. What are the typical wind speeds where you live? Is wind **energy** a good choice for your community? Why or why not?

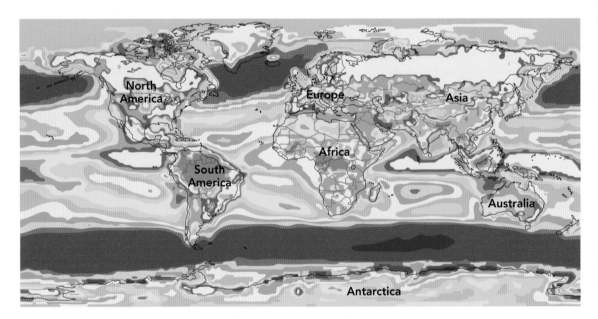

Miles per hour

| 0.0 | 2.9 | 6.0 | 7.8 | 10.0 | 11.2 | 12.3 | 13.4 | 14.5 | 15.7 | 16.8 | 17.9 | 19.0 | 20.1 | >26.8 |

| 0.0 | 1.3 | 2.7 | 3.5 | 4.5 | 5.0 | 5.5 | 6.0 | 6.5 | 7.0 | 7.5 | 8.0 | 8.5 | 9.0 | >12.0 |

Meters per second

Wind Energy Timeline

About 900	First known windmills used in Asia to pump water and grind grain. Windmills may well have been used earlier than this.
About 1100	Windmills come into use in Europe.
1400s	Windmills first used to drain wetlands so they can be used for farming in Europe.
1592	First wind-driven sawmill invented in the Netherlands.
1854	Daniel Halliday of Connecticut invents a windmill that turns to face changing wind directions and controls its own speed.
1888	First wind power plant opens in the United States.
1891	Poul la Cour of Denmark develops modern wind **turbine.**
1931	French inventor G. J. M. Darrieus invents a new kind of wind turbine called the Darrieus Turbine.
1941	Biggest windmill ever built is put up in Vermont. Its blades are 174 feet (53 meters) long. It's the first use of wind **energy** on a large scale.
1970s	Renewed interest in wind power in United States and Europe because of oil shortages.
1974	American Wind Energy Association (AWEA) founded to encourage use of wind energy.
1980s	First **wind farms** are developed in United States and Europe.
1981–1990	About 17,000 wind turbines operate in California.
1984	Canada builds the world's largest wind turbine.
1990s	India develops wind turbine program.
1991	The world's first offshore wind farm opens off the coast of Denmark.
2003	Seventy percent of the world's wind energy use is in Europe due to laws supporting its development in Germany, Denmark, and Spain. Germany leads the world in wind energy produced. In Denmark, 20 percent of all energy is produced by wind.
2007	Bahrain World Trade Center includes wind turbines in the building design.
Today	Companies are developing sails for cargo ships; research continues to make even better wind turbines.

absorb   take in and use

alternative   new or different

atmosphere   layer of gases that surround the Earth

carbon dioxide   greenhouse gas released when fossil fuels are burned

climate   general weather pattern of a region such as rain, wind, temperature, sunshine, and cloudiness throughout the year

electric grid   system of electric power lines that connect homes and businesses to a power plant

energy   ability to do work

engineer   someone who designs, constructs, or manages large building projects

fossil fuel   fuel formed millions of years ago from decayed plants and animals

fuel   something that can be burned to produce heat or power

generate   produce or create

generator   machine that produces electricity

global warming   increase in temperature of the Earth's land and water

greenhouse effect   rise in temperature on the Earth because certain gases trap energy from the sun

greenhouse gas   type of gas that traps the Earth's heat in the atmosphere. Greenhouse gases include water vapor, carbon dioxide, and methane.

hydrogen   colorless, odorless, flammable gas that combines chemically with oxygen to form water; the lightest of the known elements

hydrogen fuel cell   type of battery that uses hydrogen for energy

kinetic energy   energy of an object in motion

methane   greenhouse gas given off by burning fossil fuels

natural gases   naturally occurring gases, mostly methane, that can be used as fuel

pollute   make dirty or unclean

renewable   able to be replaced over time

rotor   rotating part of a turbine

solar energy   energy from the sun

technology   practical invention, method, or tool

turbine   engine or machine that changes one form of energy to another (often electricity)

utility-scale turbine turbine large enough to produce electricity for many homes or businesses

vertical axis wind turbine turbine that has vertical blades rather than the horizontal blades of a typical windmill

wave energy energy from waves

wind farm large group of wind turbines

Find Out More

Books

Bowden, Rob. *World About Us: Wind Energy*. North Mankato, Minn.: Stargazer, 2006.

Parker, Steve. *Wind Power*. Milwaukee: Gareth Stevens, 2004.

Sherman, Josepha. *Wind Power*. Mankato, Minn.: Capstone, 2004.

Spilsbury, Richard and Louise. *The Pros and Cons of Wind Power*. New York: Rosen, 2007.

Walker, Niki. *Generating Wind Power*. New York: Crabtree, 2007.

Websites

Energy Kids' Page
www.eia.doe.gov/kids/energyfacts/sources/renewable/wind.html

Energy Quest Games
www.energyquest.ca.gov/games/index.html

Kids' Wind Project
www.kidwind.org/materials/sciencefairideas.html

Science News for Kids
www.sciencenewsforkids.org/articles/20050309/Feature1.asp

Wind with Miller
www.windpower.org/en/kids/index.htm

Index